# · THE ·
# · ILLUSTRATED ·
# · JUNIOR ·
# · ENCYCLOPAEDIA ·
# · OF ·

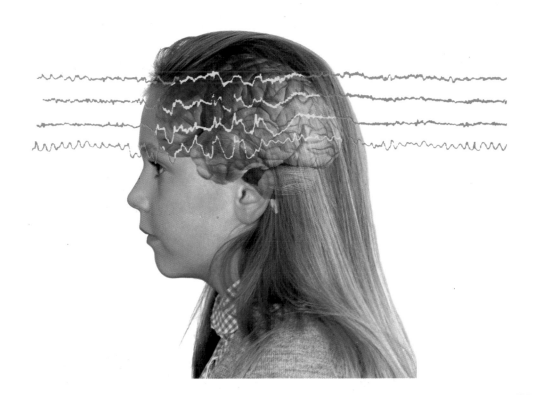

# EPILEPSY

Published in the United Kingdom by
Roby Education Ltd., 3 Lyndhurst, Maghull, Merseyside L31 6DY
for
Mersey Region Epilepsy Association
with the aid of generous financial support from Hoechst Marion Roussel Ltd.


The Illustrated Junior Encyclopaedia of Epilepsy
1st edition, 3rd reprint 1996
ISBN 0 94827060 8
© 1996 Roby Education Ltd.

Printed in the United Kingdom by the Alden Press, Oxford.

Acknowledgements
The publishers would like to thank the following for their co-operation in making this book possible:
Royal Liverpool Children's Hospital, Alder Hey; The Walton Centre for Neurology and Neurosurgery, Liverpoc
The David Lewis School, Alderley Edge; Medic Alert Foundation; Everton Football Club; Karl Drewek of
Hoechst Marion Roussel Ltd.; St. Aloysius Junior School, Huyton, Merseyside; Scientific Hospital Supplies,
Liverpool; James Appleton; Katie Byrne; Daniel Farrelly; the Finnegan family, Kate Power; Gemma Proffitt;
David Rogan, Daniel Smith.

Photographic Sources: Philip Coppell; The Image Bank, Manchester (posed by models); Science Photo Library

Dear Reader,

Every day that I go to work I meet lots of children and young people who have epilepsy. Some are babies whilst others are about to leave school and starting to think about getting a job or going to college.

It doesn't matter how clever people are, what the colour of their skin is or how rich or poor they happen to be, epilepsy does not separate one out from another. Epilepsy can affect anyone at any time.

When children come to my clinic it is my job to find out what sort of epilepsy they have and then to give medicine or tablets which will control the seizures and hopefully stop them altogether.

I couldn't do my job without a lot of help and this help comes from many different types of people. There are those who work with me in the hospital, family doctors and the companies who make the tablets. The voluntary Epilepsy Associations are groups of people who also give valuable help and support. All are there to help and so don't be afraid to ask for help if and when you need it.

This Encyclopaedia has been written to help you to learn more about epilepsy. There is no need to read it from cover to cover, although you can if you want to. Everything is organised in alphabetical order, so you can dip into any part which interests you. Perhaps the best starting point is the word "Epilepsy". Any word which is printed in pink will lead you on to another section, so you can gather all the information about any one subject.

One thing to remember is that Mums and Dads, brothers and sisters, other relations and friends and school teachers will also find this book interesting. Don't forget to let them have a look at it!

Above all, read it and enjoy it yourself.

Doctor Richard Appleton

About 20 years ago I blacked out and woke up in hospital where a nice nurse gave me a cup of tea and a chocolate biscuit. She asked me if I was frightened but I told her that I wasn't because I had slept through everything.  It's the onlookers who get worried.
After that I had a number of seizures until my doctor and I found just the right tablets for me to take.

If you have epilepsy like me, it's very important to find the right medicine (the right one for you) and to take it regularly and properly. I've found one now which tastes nice and doesn't make me sleepy.

After feeling angry when you first find out, which is only natural, you have got to settle down and make friends with your problem - after all everybody has a sensitive spot.  Some have headaches or migraines, some have athletes foot or housemaids knee or asthma and some have epilepsy. It could be a lot worse because there is so much help around for people like us these days and you do make a lot of friends.

Because I am sensitive to flickering lights, I sometimes go around the shops wearing sun glasses, even in winter. One lady came up to me and told me how fashionable I looked.  Well!!

My epilepsy has also helped me to succeed in work. Because I tackle my own problems I know what it's like to have them and this has helped me to come close to people with problems, which is nearly everyone. University makes you clever but only your problems make you wise.

My epilepsy helped me as a chaplain, a broadcaster, a writer and as a friend. In the end I think it made me grow up and become nicer than I would have been without it.

By the way, more and more big companies are welcoming people with epilepsy to come and work for them.

If you have got epilepsy you are in good company with actors, stars, company directors, writers, lots of saints, Dads, Mums and me. It has its funny side and you can use it for good.

God bless!

Rabbi Lionel Blue O.B.E.

# Absence Seizures

Absence seizures are sometimes called "petit mal" seizures.

If you had an absence seizure you would just look as though you were daydreaming. You would just stare into space, paying no attention to what is going on. You might even get told off at school for not paying attention! You would not be aware of anything that is going on in class because your brain would be "switched off" for between 5 and 15 seconds. Sometimes the eyelids flutter during an absence seizure. Absence seizures can happen lots of times a day, until somebody spots what the problem is and treats it properly with tablets or medicine. A lot of children have absence seizures.

An absence seizure is a type of generalised seizure.

# Adversive Seizures

If you had an adversive seizure your eyes or head (or both) would turn slowly to one side. If it is both, sometimes your eyes move first, followed by your head, or sometimes the head moves first. Sometimes even your whole body would follow the eyes. The eyes, head or body may turn to either the right or left side.

An adversive seizure is usually followed by another type of seizure, called a complex partial seizure, but it may also be followed by a type of seizure called a generalised seizure. It may start in the frontal lobes of the brain.

An adversive seizure is a type of simple partial seizure.

# Alexander the Great (356 - 323 B.C.)

Alexander was King of Macedon, a part of ancient Greece. Most people think he was the greatest general of ancient times. As a young prince he was extremely clever and his teacher, Aristotle, taught him how to think as a scientist. As he grew up he became interested in treating the sick, and was widely loved by the people of his country.

By the time he was 32 his kingdom stretched into Egypt and as far away as India. A huge amount of the eastern world was under his rule.

Alexandria, the second largest city in Egypt, is named after him.

The fact that he had epilepsy did not stop him from becoming one of the greatest heroes of the ancient world.

# Ambulatory E.E.G.

Sometimes an E.E.G. at the hospital shows up nothing unusual. If the doctors want to investigate further, the person might get an ambulatory E.E.G. This is an E.E.G. which is recorded whilst the person is moving about and doing things in everyday life (instead of lying down, as happens in an ordinary E.E.G.).

Electrodes (tiny wires) are fixed to the head and the leads are connected to a small cassette recorder which is carried around like a personal stereo. The E.E.G. is recorded throughout the day and night onto the cassette tape. It doesn't matter whether the person is at school, playing or watching the TV - the recording is made.

The recorded tape is then taken to the hospital and put into a computer. The computer shows the E.E.G. recording so that any problems can be noticed. This information may help the doctor in deciding what seizures might be happening and which treatment to use.

The ambulatory E.E.G. collects information 24 hours a day.

The recordings made by the ambulatory E.E.G. are checked on a computer.

## Brain Box

When somebody is having a seizure the part of the brain affected goes red. Doctors have seen this happen when people who are having brain surgery happen to have a seizure. The redness is caused by an increase in the blood flow in the affected region of the brain.

# Animals and Epilepsy

All animals have brains and so they can have epilepsy.  It is not unusual for pet dogs and cats to be treated  by a vet for epilepsy.   Obviously, animals in the wild can't visit a vet, so they can't take advantage of medicines to control seizures.

# Antiepileptic Medicine

Medicines which are used to stop epileptic seizures are called antiepileptic medicines.

Over the years, scientists and doctors have worked hard to find medicines which will control epileptic seizures. They have made a lot of progress and many very good medicines are now available to treat epilepsy. Antiepileptic medicines are also called antiepileptic drugs or anticonvulsants.

It takes many years and a great deal of money to develop antiepileptic drugs. This is because it is very important to make sure that the drugs are safe and work properly.

Choosing the best medicine for each individual person is also very important. It is just as important to make sure that it is taken regularly. If the drugs are not taken properly then they will not be able to do their job. Anyone who doesn't take the drugs as and when they are prescribed by the doctor runs a big risk of having more seizures.

Antiepileptic medicines usually come in tablets. Sometimes, however, they can be in a syrup, or in sachets containing medicine as a powder which dissolves in water to make a drink.

The medicines do not cure epilepsy but they do usually control seizures.

Some people may need to take the medicine for all of their lives while other people only have to take antiepileptic medicine when they are children. Some people seem to just grow out of it, so if they have had no seizures for a long time the doctor might think that they no longer need the medicine.

Every antiepileptic medicine has two names. One of the names is the name of the main chemical that the medicine is made from. The other name is the one used by the company which produces the drug, and is called the trade name of the drug. Sometimes the same drug is produced by more than one company, so it can have more than one trade name.

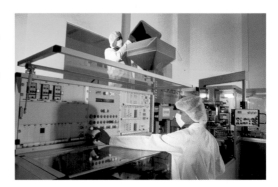

## Atonic Seizure

If you had an atonic seizure your muscles would suddenly relax and you would fall or flop to the ground. This might cause a head injury and those who have many atonic seizures sometimes have to wear protective helmets.

Atonic seizures are sometimes called "drop attacks".

An atonic seizure is a type of generalised seizure.

## Aura

This is a word which simply means "warning". It comes from a Greek word meaning "breeze".

An aura is actually a very short simple partial seizure. Some people get an aura just before they have a longer seizure, especially if it is going to be a complex partial seizure.

In children, this warning might be a strange and sometimes uncomfortable feeling in the stomach which rises into the throat, or it might even be a strange taste or smell, which can be unpleasant. Others may feel that they are "looking in on themselves" or may become aware of a familiar noise or piece of music which is not really there. One strange aura is called "deja vu" which means feeling as though you've been in exactly the same situation before - but you haven't really.

## Berger, Hans (1873 -1941)

Hans Berger was a German scientist who, in 1929, discovered that tiny electrical currents coming from the surface of the brain could be measured and recorded on a machine called an electroencephalogram (E.E.G.). This was a very important discovery and it is still used today in helping doctors to treat patients with epilepsy.

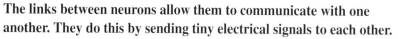

# Brain

You have to have a brain to have epilepsy.

Your brain controls every single action of your body. How clever you are, how you think, talk, hear, see, feel and move - all these things depend on your brain. It works 24 hours a day, every day!

The brain is made up of thousands of millions of cells called neurons (nerves). To give you an idea of how many neurons there are in the brain, imagine a container the size of a bath being full to the top with salt. There are still more neurons in your brain than there would be grains of salt in that bath!

As you get bigger, the number of cells in the rest of your body increases. This doesn't happen with neurons. Instead, each neuron just gets bigger and links up more and more with other neurons. In fact, as we get older the numbers of neurons actually gets smaller because a few die every day. This doesn't matter because there are so many to start with!

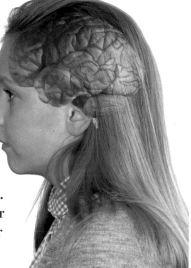

The most powerful computer in the world!

The links between neurons allow them to communicate with one another. They do this by sending tiny electrical signals to each other. The number of connections possible between all the neurons in your brain is impossible to count, just because there are so many. It is these links which make your brain far more powerful than the biggest and best computers ever invented.

Like any complicated thing, however, the brain can develop faults. Sometimes the fault could be that the electrical signals, which constantly flash backwards and forwards between the neurons, become uncontrolled, and this can cause a seizure. Many people will have at least one seizure during their lives. If they have seizures regularly then doctors say that the person has epilepsy. The type of epileptic seizure depends on the sort of fault and where it is happening in the brain. This is because the brain is organised into different parts, with each part doing different jobs.

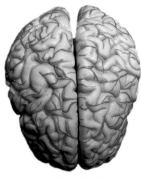

The hemispheres seen from above.

The human brain has 3 major parts - the cerebrum, the cerebellum and the brain stem.

The cerebrum, or the outside part of the brain, is divided into two halves (called hemispheres) by a deep groove. The left hemisphere controls what is happening down the right hand side of the body while the right hemisphere controls what is happening down the left hand side of the body. The two hemispheres take up 2/3 of the total weight of the brain and each one is divided into four main areas called lobes - the frontal lobes, the parietal lobes, the temporal lobes and the occipital lobes.

Although there is still a lot to be found out about the work done by the different lobes it is thought that the frontal lobes control voluntary movement; the parietal lobes control such things as touch and involuntary movement; the temporal lobes control such things as speech and hearing; and the occipital lobes control vision.

The cerebellum, which is just underneath the back of the hemispheres, makes sure that all the jobs are organised properly and that everything works together in the correct way and at the right time. It is particularly important for how we balance on our feet.

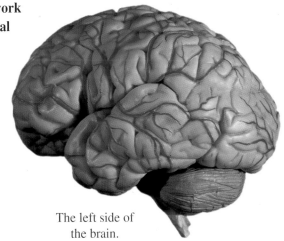

The left side of the brain.

Right underneath the hemispheres is the brain stem which controls important jobs like breathing and heartbeat. It also 'joins' the brain with the spinal cord. The brain stem was the first part of the brain to develop or evolve - it existed even in the prehistoric apes, which are our distant ancestors.

No one part of the brain is entirely responsible for any one job. All the parts are interconnected and share each others work. The human brain is still the most wonderful and complicated thing that we know about in the whole universe.

*Cerebrum*

*Pituitary gland*

*Brain stem*

*Cerebellum*

Cross-section of the brain showing some of the main areas.

# BC

## Brain Mapping

This is a special way of using E.E.G.s. The E.E.G.s are fed into a very special computer to try to find out exactly where the seizure may be starting in the brain. Most children don't need this test.

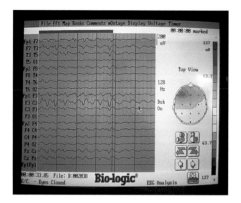

The screen of the brain mapping computer.

## Caesar, Julius (100 - 44 B.C.)

Julius Caesar was one of the greatest generals who ever lived - he was extremely clever and courageous. One writer described him as a superman and genius for the way he led the Roman Empire.

Caesar arrived on the shores of Britain in the year 54 BC . His invasion made him a great hero in the city of Rome. He remained the world's most powerful man until March, 44 BC when he was stabbed to death by a group of men led by Brutus and Cassius.

Throughout his life he kept in very good health. The fact that he had epilepsy didn't affect his success in any way.

## Carbamazepine

Carbamazepine is the name of the chemical used in the drug Tegretol® and also Tegretol Retard®.

See Antiepileptic Medicines.

## Careers

Nearly every type of job is open to people with epilepsy. There are a few, however, which would be unsuitable and it is better to know which these are before deciding what sort of work to look for after leaving school.

A lot of young people, with a well controlled epilepsy, leave school to study at colleges and universities. After finishing their studies they start work where they have to use their brains more than their hands. Lots get jobs as doctors, nurses, civil servants, lawyers and teachers. The list is endless.

Other people learn skills which allow them to work in factories, shops or perhaps outside. A well controlled epilepsy should be no problem for most jobs. For example there are international sports stars who have epilepsy and they haven't let it get in the way of reaching the very top in their own sports.

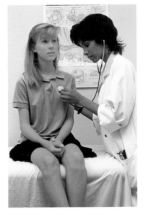

The jobs which are not open to people with epilepsy include driving heavy lorries or buses, trains, aeroplanes etc.

A person with epilepsy would have great difficulty in joining the army, navy, air force, fire brigade or the police force. It would not be a good idea for somebody with epilepsy to become a deep sea diver or a scaffolder.

As long as these jobs are avoided, young people with epilepsy can have a very successful and satisfying career.

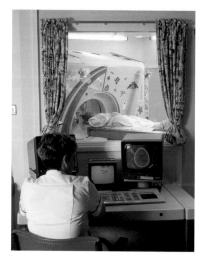

# CAT Scanner

A CAT scan is a special type of X-ray machine.

CAT stands for Computer Assisted Tomography.

When doctors need clear pictures of the brain they can use X-Rays. Ordinary X-ray machines aren't much use for this. A CAT Scanner takes a few X-Ray pictures and then feeds them into a computer. The computer makes very clear, detailed pictures of the brain, rather like cross-sections.

The radiographer operates the CAT scanner.

A specialised doctor (called a radiologist) looks at these pictures for any problems.

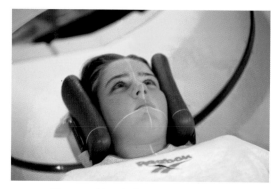

The machine is lined up accurately using rays of light.

To have a CAT Scan you lie down on a type of bed, which is moved by an operator (called a radiographer) so that your head is surrounded by the special X-ray scanner. You have to lie still until the machine has finished the job. It only takes a few minutes. There is no pain and it is not at all uncomfortable.

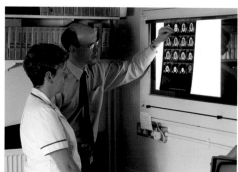

Most important of all, it is quite safe.

Most children with epilepsy do not need to have a CAT Scan.

The radiographer and doctor examine the scans.

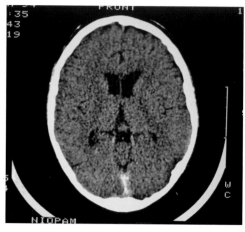

A CAT scan of a cross-section of the brain.

# Climbing

This is not a good idea if you have epilepsy. Scrambling across low objects is no problem, but climbing up trees, cliffs and mountains can be dangerous. If you lose consciousness in a seizure, whilst half way up a tree or a ladder, there is only one way that you are going to go and that is downwards! The problems which that can cause are obvious. It is far better not to climb than to finish up in hospital with broken bones or perhaps serious head injuries.

# Clobazam

Clobazam is the name of the chemical used in the drug Frisium®.

See Antiepileptic Medicines.

# Clonazepam

Clonazepam is the name of the chemical used in the drug Rivotril®.

See Antiepileptic Medicines.

# Clonic Seizures

The word clonic comes from the word "clonus" which means to contract or to relax. If you had a clonic seizure then muscles in your body would contract, relax, contract again and so on. This would cause you to jerk or twitch repeatedly.

Clonic seizures are types of convulsion.

A clonic seizure is a type of generalised seizure.

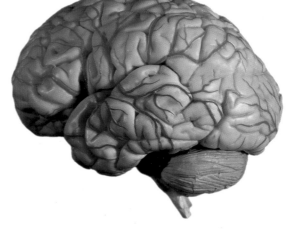

# Complex Partial Seizures

These types of seizure happen when one part of the brain, usually a part called the temporal lobe, doesn't behave as it should do. Complex partial seizures are different from generalised seizures because only part of the brain is involved in partial seizures - not the whole brain. However, although a complex partial seizure may start in one part of the brain it can then go on to affect the whole brain. When this happens it is called a secondarily generalised seizure. They are different from the other main type of partial seizure, simple partial seizures, because in complex partial seizures the person is not fully conscious.

There are two temporal lobes, one on the left side and one on the right side of the brain. They are very

Complex partial seizures start here.

complicated and control such things as our memory and our senses of smell and taste. They also organise our sense of timing and such things as our understanding of music. Imagine the problems when a temporal lobe fails to work properly.

If you have epilepsy which involves complex partial seizures, the start may be a funny feeling in your tummy which rises up into the throat. You might have a funny taste in your mouth or think that there is a strange smell or you might even believe that there is a familiar piece of music being played. Such feelings are called auras but in fact they are seizures in themselves.

## Brain Box

The left hemisphere (side) of your brain controls the right hand side of your body, and the right hemisphere controls the left hand side. In most people, messages from the left hemisphere override messages from the right hemisphere, so most people (about 9 out of every 10) are right handed. Nobody is really sure why this is.

After the aura you might behave in strange ways by smacking your lips or plucking at your clothes. You might wander about the room without any purpose and appear confused or dazed. Complex partial seizures are sometimes called temporal lobe epilepsy. These seizures can last anything from a few seconds up to a few hours.

Complex partial seizures can also start in the frontal lobes. When they happen there they may cause adversive seizures.

# Compliance

To be compliant simply means that you do as you are asked.

When doctors use the word "compliance" they are talking about their patients taking their medicines properly - in other words, the right dose at the right time. The sensible thing to do to avoid having seizures is to do as the doctor tells you. This is very important because medicine and tablets only work if they are taken regularly every day and not just when you feel like it. Sometimes people stop taking their medicines because they haven't had a seizure for a long time. This is, of course, a big mistake - it is the medicines that are stopping the seizures!

# Convulsion

A convulsion is when the muscles of the body move out of control. All the muscles of the body can become stiff and then jerk. This can involve the arms, legs and face. This can last for between 2 and 5 minutes. Very occasionally it can last for longer. If this happens doctors call it status epilepticus.

When the bladder is full and the muscles controlling it contract, people having convulsions sometimes wet themselves.

Limbs move out of control
during a convulsion.

A convulsion can look frightening to those who have never seen one before. People having convulsions which affect the whole body are unconscious and do not feel a thing. They are not painful.

Many people with epilepsy do have convulsions. The most common type of epilepsy with convulsions is called 'grand mal' epilepsy. The correct name for grand mal seizures is tonic-clonic seizures.

When people use the word convulsion, they are usually talking about a tonic-clonic seizure. It is possible, however, for somebody to have convulsions which don't affect the whole body. The convulsions might just affect one side of the body. In these cases, the person doesn't always lose consciousness during the convulsions.

# CD

## Cycling

Many children are told that they can't ride a bicycle because they have epilepsy. This is not correct. Children with epilepsy can ride bicycles provided that they ride them in safe areas. What they must not do is to ride them on busy roads where there is danger from traffic. Everybody should wear a helmet when riding a bicycle, not just people with epilepsy.

## Diving

A trip to the swimming pool is great fun, and all children should learn to swim whether they have got epilepsy or not. Diving boards can be dangerous for people with epilepsy because if they have a seizure and fall from the diving board they can suffer serious injury or fall on somebody else.

## Dostoevsky, Fyodor (1821 - 1881)

Fyodor Dostoevsky was born in Moscow, the capital of Russia. After leaving school, he joined the army and became an engineer. He disliked army life, and, when he left, he took up writing books, something he had always wanted to do.

He wrote many short stories and articles in magazines but he is most famous for his books. His most famous books are "The Idiot" and "The Devils". In some of his books he wrote about his epilepsy.

Experts say that he was one of the greatest story tellers that ever lived.

## Driving

Most young people look forward to the day when they can drive a car, and it is no different for those with epilepsy. People with epilepsy can qualify for a driving licence if they have been free from seizures for at least one year. If they have seizures, but only while they are asleep, they can still qualify, as long as there have been no daytime seizures for the previous 3 years. The details of the rules and regulations can be obtained from the Epilepsy Associations.

It can be very difficult, however, for a person with epilepsy to obtain a licence to drive LGVs (large goods vehicles) or PCVs (passenger carrying vehicles).

## Drop Attacks

**See** "Atonic Seizures"

## E.E.G. - electroencephalogram

This is a machine which is used to record the tiny amounts of electricity given off by the brain.

Wires, called electrodes, are attached to your head, sometimes using a rubber net or by a special glue.

The brainwaves, which the brain gives off all the time, are picked up by the electrodes and fed into the machine. A picture of these brainwaves is traced onto a piece of paper for doctors to study. The tracings are called an electroencephalograph. The letters E.E.G. also stand for electroencephalograph!

At some time during the test, the E.E.G. operator will flash lights in your eyes (this is to look for photosensitivity). You will also be asked to blow at a tissue in order to breathe quickly (this is called hyperventilation).

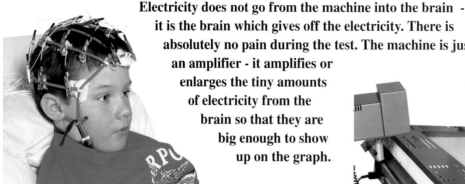

Electricity does not go from the machine into the brain - it is the brain which gives off the electricity. There is absolutely no pain during the test. The machine is just an amplifier - it amplifies or enlarges the tiny amounts of electricity from the brain so that they are big enough to show up on the graph.

## E.E.G. - electroencephalograph

This is a trace of the brainwaves recorded by the electroencephalogram. Each line on the graph gives a picture of the brainwaves being produced by a different part of the brain.

Sometimes, although a person has epilepsy, the E.E.G. does not pick up any epileptic type patterns. In this case, the person might be asked to wear an ambulatory E.E.G. for a while.

The doctor studies the E.E.G. traces.

This is a normal E.E.G. trace. The trace changes towards the right because the eyes were opened for a short while.

This is a trace showing a generalised seizure. The brainwaves are abnormal over the whole of the brain for the short spell of this seizure (an absence seizure in this case).

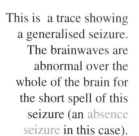

## Education

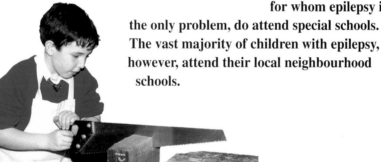

By law, all children have to receive a full education to prepare them for later life. They must study the National Curriculum and children with epilepsy are no exception.

If you have epilepsy then, as a rule, you can take part in all lessons taught in a school and are expected to do homework when it is set. You are treated as a normal child who just happens to have epilepsy.

Having epilepsy is no excuse for not working hard. By the time you reach the age of 16 years you should be educated well enough to live confidently as an adult.

Some children with severe epilepsy, or perhaps those for whom epilepsy is not the only problem, do attend special schools. The vast majority of children with epilepsy, however, attend their local neighbourhood schools.

## Emeside®

Emeside® is a trade name for the drug ethosuximide. It is taken as soft orange capsules or as a syrup which can be blackcurrant or orange flavoured. It is used in the treatment of absence seizures and, occasionally, myoclonic seizures.

See Antiepileptic Medicines.

## Epanutin®

Epanutin® is the trade name for the drug phenytoin. It is taken as capsules or as cherry red syrup. It is used in the treatment of both generalised and partial seizures.

See Antiepileptic Medicines.

# Epilepsy

As long as there have been men and women on earth there have been those with epilepsy. The word "epilepsy" comes from a Greek word meaning "to take hold of". In ancient times it used to be called "the falling sickness". In those days this was a good description because people thought that there was only one type of seizure - the person fell to the ground and had convulsions. These days we would call these tonic-clonic seizures.

Today, however, we know a lot more about epilepsy and have learned that there are many different types of epileptic seizures. The term "falling sickness" is no longer used.

Epilepsy is not a disease - it is just a symptom that part of the brain is not always working normally. When the brain is working normally it gives off tiny amounts of well organised electricity. Electricity pylons carry electricity around the country in a well organised way, just like the neurons in the brain when everything is working normally. However, when somebody is having a seizure the electricity becomes very disorganised - a bit like flashes of lightning during a thunderstorm. The type of seizure a person has depends on the place in the brain where the "storm" happens.

Epilepsy is a condition where a person has a series of seizures. A single "one off" seizure is not epilepsy - at least two or three seizures must have occurred before a doctor will label the condition as epilepsy. A great many people will have a single seizure at some point during their lives, but this won't be epilepsy.

It is thought that at least one person in every two hundred has got epilepsy. This means that in Britain alone there are at least 100,000 children with epilepsy - more than enough to fill a large football ground, like Everton's Goodison Park shown here, nearly 3 times over! Every day you are bound to pass at least one person who has epilepsy, whether you know it or not. Most schools have more than one pupil with epilepsy. Epilepsy is very common, so it is hard to understand why so many people know so little about it.

# E Epilepsy Associations

These are voluntary groups of people who work hard to make life as good as possible for people with epilepsy. Epilepsy Associations offer all sorts of support such as setting up groups of people with an interest in epilepsy, producing leaflets and providing expert help for parents and children who live with epeilepsy every day. They also raise money to help scientists and doctors find out more about the condition and come up with better treatments.

There are 5 main Associations working in Great Britain and Ireland. Their telephone numbers are listed on the page opposite.

# Fit

**This is the old-fashioned word for a** seizure **or** convulsion**.**

# Focal Motor Seizures

**The word 'focal' comes from 'focus' which means centre point, and 'motor' means movement. Put the two together to get 'movement from a centre point'. If, therefore, the point of the** brain **which controls the movement of the left arm goes out of order then that arm will move out of control. So it is with other parts of the body. This movement is, in fact, an epileptic** seizure. **A focal motor seizure is a type of** simple partial seizure**.**

# Focal Sensory Seizures

**The word 'focal' comes from 'focus' which means centre point and 'sensory' means 'feeling'. Put the two together to get 'feeling from a centre point'. So, if the part of the** brain **which looks after such feelings as tingling in the fingers goes out of order then the person will get a tingling feeling in the fingers. These feelings are, in fact, an epileptic** seizure. **A focal sensory seizure is a type of** simple partial seizure**.**

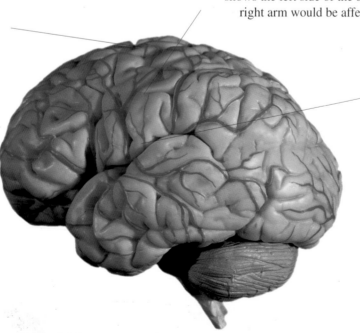

Focal seizures starting here would affect the legs (since this picture shows the left side of the brain, the right leg would be affected.)

Focal seizures starting here will affect the arms (since this picture shows the left side of the brain, the right arm would be affected.)

Focal seizures starting here will affect the face.

Let the person have a sleep or at least a good rest.

## NEVER FORCE ANYTHING IN THE MOUTH DURING THE SEIZURE

Some people wrongly think that you need to do this in order to prevent the person's tongue getting bitten. The worst that can happen with a bitten tongue is that it will hurt for a day or two - it heals very quickly. The worst that can happen if something is forced in the mouth is that teeth will get badly broken - these will never heal.

**IF ONE SEIZURE FOLLOWS ANOTHER WITHOUT THE PERSON REGAINING CONSCIOUSNESS, OR IF A SEIZURE LASTS LONGER THAN 5 MINUTES, GET HELP IMMEDIATELY.**

# First Aid

There are very few things which have to be done to help someone who is having a convulsive seizure. These are:

Move objects out of the way which could hurt the person having the seizure.
In the photograph the coffee table is being moved so that the girl will not bang her head against any hard or sharp edges.

If possible, place something under the person's head so that the head doesn't bang against the floor, causing injury.
In the photograph a cushion is being used, but a rolled up coat or jumper would do just as well.

Let the seizure run its course. When it is over move the person to a comfortable place. Sometimes the person needs to be carried because of extreme tiredness, but usually only a little help is needed.

# Epilepsy Association Telephone Numbers

A. **British Epilepsy Association (Leeds)**  0800 309030

B. **Epilepsy Association of Scotland (Glasgow)**  0141 427 4911

C. **Irish Epilepsy Association (Dublin)**  Dublin 4557500

D. **Mersey Region Epilepsy Association (Liverpool)**  0151 298 2666

E. **National Society for Epilepsy (Chalfont St. Peter)**  01494 873991

## Epilepsy Nurse

In some hospitals there are nurses who are specially trained to help people with epilepsy. These nurses work in both children's hospitals and in adult's hospitals. They help people to get the best out of life even though they might have epilepsy. Very often the epilepsy nurse will explain a lot about epilepsy to people such as teachers and other nurses, who are working with children who have seizures, so that they understand what is happening and how best to help.

## Epilim®

Epilim® is a trade name for the drug sodium valproate. It is taken as lilac-coloured coated, or plain white tablets. It can also be taken as a red cherry flavoured liquid. It is used to treat all types of generalised seizures and partial seizures.

See Antiepileptic Medicines.

## Ethosuximide

Ethosuximide is the name of the chemical used in the drugs Emeside® and Zarontin®.

See Antiepileptic Medicines.

## Frisium®

Frisium® is a trade name for the drug clobazam. It is rarely used in the treatment of epilepsy but is sometimes taken along with another antiepileptic drug. It comes in capsules or, rarely, as a tablet or special liquid. See Antiepileptic Medicines.

## Frontal Lobes

These are the parts of the brain at the front of the head, just behind the forehead.

The job of the frontal lobes is still something of a mystery, but scientists think that they may have something to do with personality, and perhaps with how we plan things.

Sometimes a seizure can start from inside a frontal lobe and give rise to complex partial seizures and adversive seizures.

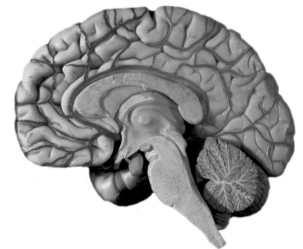

## Gabapentin

Gabapentin is the name of the chemical used in the drug Neurontin®.

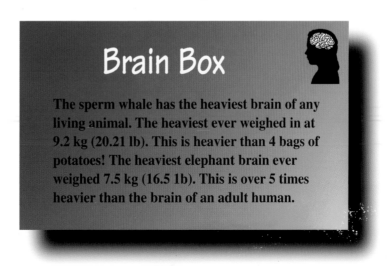

## Brain Box

The sperm whale has the heaviest brain of any living animal. The heaviest ever weighed in at 9.2 kg (20.21 lb). This is heavier than 4 bags of potatoes! The heaviest elephant brain ever weighed 7.5 kg (16.5 1b). This is over 5 times heavier than the brain of an adult human.

## Generalised Seizures

In this type of seizure the whole brain is affected by the electrical disturbance. People having a generalised seizure are completely unaware of what is going on because they are unconscious. Types of generalised epilepsy are: tonic-clonic seizures, absence seizures, myoclonic/jerk seizures, atonic (drop attacks), and clonic seizures. Seizures which aren't generalised are called partial seizures. Generalised seizures are different from partial seizures because the whole brain is involved. Only part of the brain is affected in partial seizures.

## Grand Mal Seizures

See Tonic-clonic Seizures.

## Guanarius, Antonius

Antonius Guanarius lived in the 16th century and was one of the first doctors to study epilepsy. He advised people how to avoid seizures and also gave first aid advice. His methods were very strange and quite useless although he meant well.

He recommended that on seeing a person having a seizure the onlooker should kill a dog and give the bile to the patient. This, he said, would make the patient completely well.

The tablets for preventing seizures were to be made from the rib of a man who had been hanged or beheaded. These were to be taken with water!

You won't be surprised to know that neither of these cures made the slightest difference (except to the dog!)

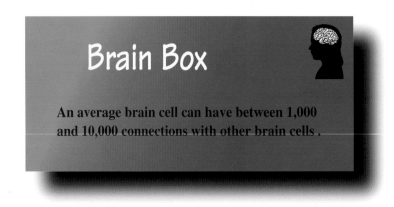

## Brain Box

An average brain cell can have between 1,000 and 10,000 connections with other brain cells .

## Brain Box

Throughout the world there are about 30 million people who have epilepsy. Compare this with the population of the United Kingdom - about 57 million.

Epilepsy is very common indeed.

# Hammurabi, Code of

Hammurabi was King of Babylon. He ruled his kingdom using laws which were carved on to a long stone pillar and placed in the Hanging Gardens of Babylon. He called this his Code.

Two of his laws were for people with epilepsy. One was that people with epilepsy were not allowed to marry. The other said that they were not allowed to appear in a court of law, either as a witness or as a member of a jury.

He thought that these were good laws but really they were very unfair. The problem was that he didn't understand epilepsy. He thought that if people with epilepsy got married and had children then the children would have epilepsy too. He also thought that people with epilepsy were not clever enough to judge other people. In other words he didn't know what he was talking about!

The actual stone pillar can be seen today at the Louvre Museum in Paris.

# H

## Handel, George Frederick (1685 - 1759)

George Frederick Handel was one of the world's most brilliant and best loved musicians. He was born in Germany and when he was very young his parents noticed his love of music. His father wanted him to be a lawyer but Handel just wanted to write and play music. He left Germany and moved to England, where he continued writing his wonderful music.

Two of his most famous works are "The Messiah" and "Water Music".

This great genius, who had epilepsy, is buried in Westminster Abbey.

## Hauptman, Alfred

In 1912 this German scientist discovered that the drug phenobarbitone was very good at preventing seizures. It was the first real breakthrough in treating people with epilepsy. Many thousands of people with epilepsy started to take the drug and it improved their lives tremendously.

## Headaches

Everybody at some time or other has a headache. People with epilepsy, for various reasons, can have more headaches than others. Very often a person can complain of a severe headache after a tonic-clonic seizure. Fortunately this usually goes away after a good rest or sleep.

## Brain Box

Some of the chemical reactions that take place in the brain take only 1 millionth of a second to happen.

## Hemisphere

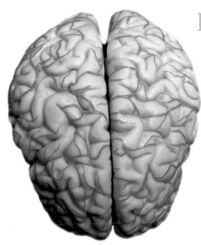

A hemisphere is part of the brain. Every brain has two hemispheres. The two hemispheres are not totally separated. They are joined together by a thick bundle of nerves called the corpus callosum. The left hemisphere controls the right hand side of the body, while the right hemisphere controls the left side.

Partial or focal seizures may start in either of the two hemispheres (the whole hemisphere may be affected or just one part of the hemisphere).

## Hippocrates, "The Greek Father of Medicine" (460 - 377 B.C.)

Sitting under a plane tree on the Greek island of Kos, Hippocrates taught his students about causes and treatment of sickness. One of the disorders he studied closely was epilepsy. In those days, many people thought that epilepsy had something to do with the position of the Moon! Hippocrates taught that this wasn't true. Also, he said that epilepsy was nothing to do with being possessed by the devil, which many people had previously believed. He taught his students that epilepsy was caused by something going wrong in the brain. His explanation was that epilepsy was due to an excess of liquid in the brain. The explanation was wrong but nevertheless he was the first person to link epilepsy with brain disorder. All his work on epilepsy was published in his writings called "On the Sacred Disease".

# H

## Hyperventilation

**Hyperventilation means overbreathing.**

Some children's seizures are brought on by breathing too deeply or too quickly. This causes sudden changes in the amounts of carbon dioxide and oxygen in the bloodstream. The body often cannot cope with these changes and, if the person has 'petit mal' epilepsy, there is a chance that an absence seizure will happen. Overbreathing does not usually bring on a tonic-clonic or partial seizure.

Blowing on a tissue to see if this causes a seizure.

During an E.E.G. test, children, particularly younger ones, are asked to blow rapidly at a tissue held in front of them. This is to see if there is any change in the pattern of the graph being printed. If the blowing brings on an absence seizure then obviously the child can't blow any more while the seizure is happening (because he or she is unconscious) and the tissue remains still. The doctor knows to look at the E.E.G. machine to see the result of the electrical disturbance on the graph paper.

Don't overdo it!

## Brain Box

The brain of an adult man weighs about 1.4 kg. The heaviest human brain ever weighed over 2.2kg.

The size of your brain has nothing to do with how clever you are.

# I

## IBE

These are the initials of the "International Bureau for Epilepsy" which tries to improve public understanding of epilepsy throughout the world.

## Idiopathic Epilepsy

This term is used to describe epilepsy with no known cause.

Doctors try very hard to find out what might be causing epileptic seizures. If no obvious cause can be found, the epilepsy is called idiopathic epilepsy. Most people who have epilepsy have an idiopathic epilepsy.

## ILAE

These are the initials of the "International League Against Epilepsy" which is an organisation of doctors, with members all over the world. It tries to help doctors to find better treatments for epilepsy.

## Infantile Spasms

Infantile spasms are a severe type of epilepsy which usually happen between the ages of 3 and 10 months. The seizures are sometimes called "Salaam Attacks". The infant's head bends forward suddenly and with force, while the arms and the knees bend or straighten very quickly. Each spasm lasts a second or less. These seizures or spasms may happen many times a day. Adults who see this happening often just think that the baby has wind or 'colic'.

# JK

## Jackson, John Hughlings (1835 - 1911)

John Hughlings Jackson is known as the "Father of English Neurology". He became interested in epilepsy because of his wife. She would be quite relaxed and for no apparent reason her thumb would start twitching. He realised that she was having some sort of epileptic seizure and so he gathered information about other people who had the same type of problem. He found out that some epilepsies start with a movement in a particular part of the body and can spread to other parts. These seizures usually start in the fingers and then spread up the hand, arm and into the face. Other doctors agreed with his findings and called these movement seizures "Jacksonian Epilepsy". Jacksonian seizures often start in a frontal lobe. Today they are called "focal motor seizures".

## Ketogenic diet

This is food which is rich in fat and oils. Ketogenic diets are sometimes recommended when seizures are not controlled properly by drugs. People are only allowed to eat what is in this diet, which includes the liquids in the bottles shown here. It is occasionally successful but is not a very pleasant diet.

## Brain Box

Every nerve cell in your brain is linked up with many others. There are so many connections between all the cells in your brain that if you started counting them now, one every second, you would finish in 32 million years time!

L

## Lamictal®

Lamictal® is the trade name for the drug lamotrigine. It is taken as yellow tablets which may be swallowed whole or crushed and is used alone or with other drugs in the treatment of partial seizures and generalised tonic-clonic, absences and myoclonic seizures.

See Antiepileptic Medicines.

## Lamotrigine

Lamotrigine is the name of the chemical used in the drug Lamictal®.

See Antiepileptic Medicines.

## Lennox-Gastaut Syndrome

This type of epilepsy usually begins between the ages of 1 and 5 years and rarely after the age of 8 years. It is named after two doctors called Lennox and Gastaut, who did a lot of research into epilepsy in children. Children with this Lennox-Gastaut Syndrome have seizures of different kinds, and so it is a condition which is difficult to treat. The kinds of seizures which occur include tonic, atonic, tonic-clonic and myoclonic seizures. Children (and adults) with this type of epilepsy may have status epilepticus.

Children with this type of epilepsy usually have some learning difficulties and may have to go to a special school.

### Brain Box

A new born baby has more brain cells than a university professor. The reason why an adult's brain is bigger than a child's brain is because it fills up with other types of supporting cells - not brain cells.

Throughout our lives we lose brain cells - and unlike cells in other parts of our bodies, they never get replaced. Adults lose thousands of brain cells every day - luckily humans have so many to start with that this has no effect on us.

# M

## Medic Alert

People with epilepsy usually carry some form of identification to explain what sort of epilepsy they have and what sort of help they need should they have a seizure. This information can either be on a simple card, or can be included on a piece of jewellery such as a necklace or bracelet. An example of such jewellery is a Medic Alert. Information about the person's epilepsy, together with a special telephone number and identification number, are engraved on the back of the jewellery. Full details of Medic Alert's jewellery can be obtained from the Medic Alert Foundation (telephone 0171 833 3034)

## MRI Scanner

An MRI scanner produces extremely clear and detailed pictures of the brain. It doesn't use X-Rays like a CAT scanner. MRI stands for Magnetic Resonance Imaging.

If you had this test you would have to lie still for a few minutes, surrounded by what looks like a CAT scanner. The test is done very quickly and you wouldn't feel a thing.

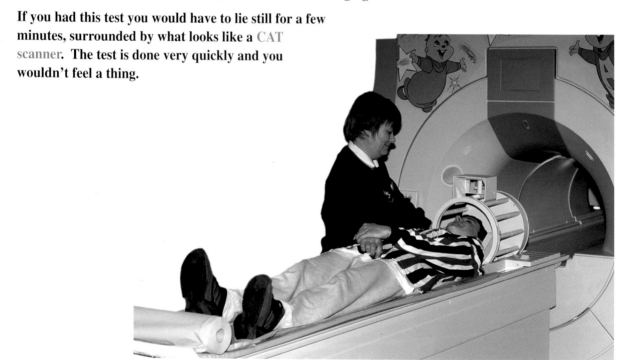

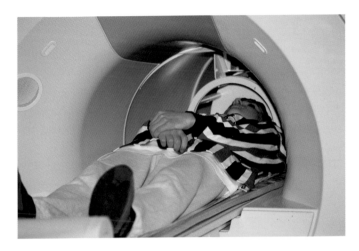

The doctor studies the pictures to see if there is anything in the brain causing the person to have seizures. If the problem can be seen, sometimes it can be treated and, hopefully, the seizures will cease. Very often, nothing at all is found.

Only a small number of children with epilepsy will need to have an MRI Scan.

A close-up picture of a boy having an MRI scan. Unlike an E.E.G. machine, there are no wires.

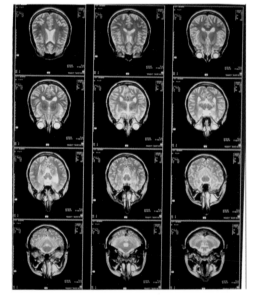

This picture shows a series of MRI scans through a person's head, as if seen from above. The front of the head is at the bottom of each little picture, and they are all different because each scan looks at a different level. The brain can be seen in each scan, while the eyeballs are clearly visible in a few of them.

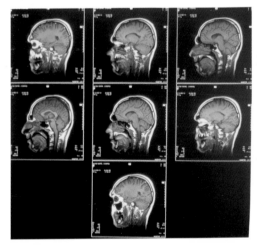

These scans are taken as if from the left side of the head. Again, they are all different because they show different levels.

# MN

## Myoclonic Seizures

"Myo" means muscle and "clonic" means jerk. So when a myoclonic seizure happens the muscles jerk. These jerks may look like sudden electric shocks and may cause the person to fall. The most usual jerks happen in the arms and very often they happen early in the morning, just after waking, or in the evening before bedtime when the person is starting to get tired. The person having the seizure loses consciousness, but does not seem to do so because the seizure is so short. A myoclonic seizure is a type of generalised seizure.

## Napoleon (1762 - 1821)

Napoleon Bonaparte was a military genius who became Emperor of France. He was born in Corsica and, after joining the French army, was promoted quickly because he was very clever and everybody could see that he was a good leader.

After marrying his wife Josephine in 1796 he led his soldiers into battle against the armies of Prussia (now part of Germany), Austria and Italy and had great success. He was crowned Emperor of France in 1804.

After many years of power his army was defeated in Russia - not by soldiers, but by extremely bad weather. The conditions left his troops unable to fight because they were too cold and hungry.

His reign came to an end in 1815 when he was defeated at the Battle of Waterloo.

Napoleon is a great example of how people with epilepsy can get to the very top.

# Nervous System

Your nervous system links together all the nerves in your body. Nerves from all over your body are gathered together in the spinal cord and their electrical messages are carried to your brain. Nerve cells are sometimes called neurons.

The body's nervous system is divided into two parts - the central nervous system and the peripheral nervous system.

The central nervous system, centred in the brain, controls such things as memory, thought and understanding. It receives messages from nerves outside the brain and organises them before sending the organised message back.

The peripheral nervous system is that part of the system which is outside the head and spinal cord. It is split into three major parts - the motor system, the sensory system and the autonomic system.

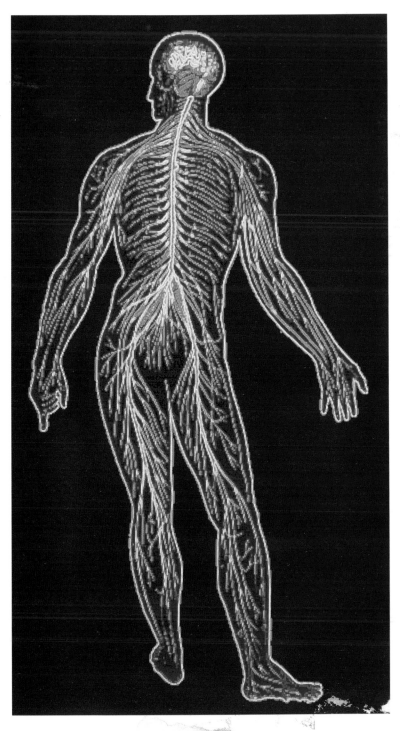

The brain and spinal cord make up the central nervous system (yellow/orange in this picture). There are 31 pairs of nerves that branch off the spinal cord. These carry nerve impulses from the central nervous system to the various parts of the body, and back again. Nerves which are not part of the central nervous system (light blue) are part of the peripheral nervous sytem.

The motor system is responsible for the movement of the muscles. For example, when we walk the nerves in the muscles of the legs are sending messages back to the brain which then organises these messages to make sure that the muscles move correctly and we walk in a straight line. If a person drinks too much the alcohol affects the workings of the brain. The messages going back to the nerves in the legs are not organised properly and so it is not possible to walk in a straight line.

The sensory nervous system is responsible for senses and feelings. The brain organises messages sent from the eye so that we see clear pictures, messages sent from the ear so that we hear clearly, messages which give the ability to enjoy the sweet scent of a flower, to learn through touch and to enjoy the taste of the food we eat.

The autonomic nervous system is responsible for the automatic workings of the body . For example, as the body sleeps the nerves connected to the breathing system continue to work and keep us alive. When we eat, the nerves in the digestive system work without us knowing to make sure that we get all the goodness out of our food. The autonomic nervous system also makes us sweat (when we are too hot) and shiver (when we are too cold).

Seizures happen when neurons in the brain give off haphazard electricity instead of organised messages. Since the brain is the part of the nervous system that controls everything else it is easy to see why a seizure can cause a person's body to go out of control.

## Neurologist

This is the name given to a doctor who specialises in treating disorders of the brain and the nervous system. Some of these doctors have a particular interest in epilepsy and advise other hospital doctors and family doctors how best to treat people's epilepsy. They treat adults, rather than children, since the children have specialists of their own called paediatric neurologists.

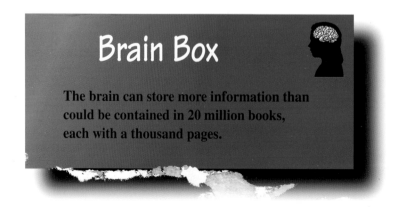

### Brain Box

The brain can store more information than could be contained in 20 million books, each with a thousand pages.

# Neuron

The body is made out of tiny parts called cells. The cells that make up the brain and nervous system are called neurons. Neurons are far too small to be seen without a microscope.

Neurons have a main part, called the cell body, and a long tail, called the axon. There are short tails branching off the axon, called dendrites. The axon acts like a sort of wire, carrying messages.

A neuron's dendrites attach themselves to other neurons, making an incredibly complicated network. This complicated network allows the messages from one neuron to be received by many others. Messages travel from neuron to neuron along the axon and dendrites in the form of tiny electrical pulses. If these electrical pulses get badly out of control, or out of the correct sequence, then a seizure occurs.

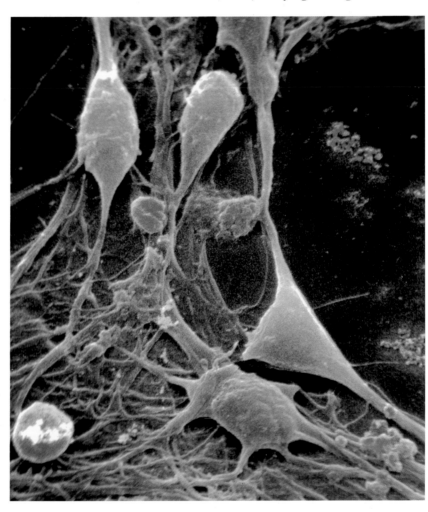

This is a highly magified image (almost 1000 times) of neurons from the cerebral cortex (known as the cerebrum - the outer part of the brain). The main cell body of each neuron is visible, as well as the axon. A mesh of smaller dendrites is also visible.

# Neurontin®

Neurontin® is the trade name for the drug gabapentin. It is taken as capsules which are either white, yellow or orange depending on the strength, and is used to treat partial and secondarily generalised seizures.

See Antiepileptic Medicines.

# NP

## Neurosurgeon

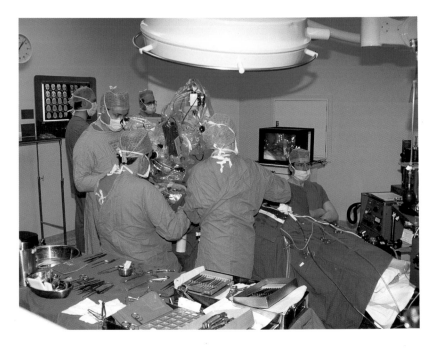

This is the name given to a doctor who operates on the brain or nervous system. Many people call them brain surgeons, but neurosurgeons can operate on any part of the body that has nerves. Only a small number of all those who have seizures can be helped by an operation.

## Nocturnal Seizures

These are seizures that people have when they are asleep. The word nocturnal means "night time" and so, because most people sleep during the night time, it is a good word to describe the seizures.

## Paediatric Neurologist

Paediatric neurologists are doctors who specialise in treating disorders of children's nervous systems. Some of these doctors have a great interest in epilepsy and are experts at treating children who have seizures. They advise other hospital doctors and family doctors how to treat children with epilepsy.

# Partial Seizures

Only part of the body is affected by these seizures. The part of the body affected depends on which part of the brain is having the disturbance. Partial seizures are different from generalised seizures because only part of the brain is affected by partial seizures. In generalised seizures the whole brain is affected right from the start of the seizure. Partial seizures may go on to involve the whole brain - it is then called a secondarily generalised seizure.

There are two main types of partial seizures - simple partial seizures and complex partial seizures. The brain is organised into main areas called lobes. These are shown in the diagram, along with the effects that a partial seizure in that part of the brain might have.

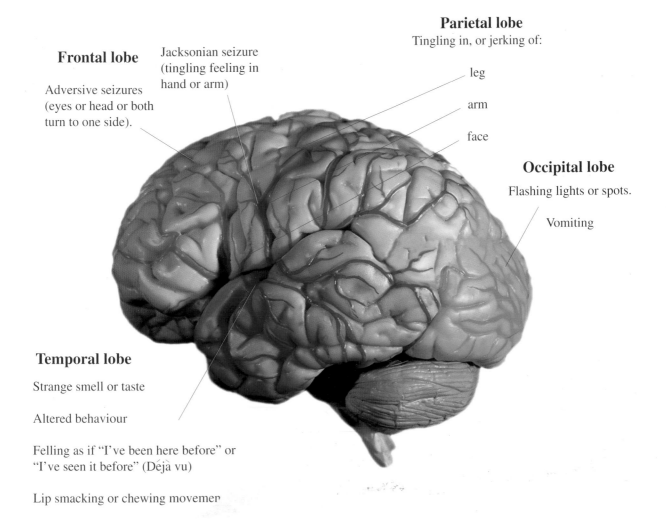

**Parietal lobe**
Tingling in, or jerking of:

leg

arm

face

**Frontal lobe**

Jacksonian seizure (tingling feeling in hand or arm)

Adversive seizures (eyes or head or both turn to one side).

**Occipital lobe**

Flashing lights or spots.

Vomiting

**Temporal lobe**

Strange smell or taste

Altered behaviour

Felling as if "I've been here before" or "I've seen it before" (Déjà vu)

Lip smacking or chewing movemen

# P

## Petit Mal Epilepsy

**See** Absence Seizures

## Phenobarbitone

This was one of the first drugs that successfully treated epilepsy. It was first used in 1912 by Alfred Hauptman to control seizures and some older people today take it for their epilepsy. It is very unusual for children to be given phenobarbitone before other drugs have been tried. There are some children, however, who take it because other drugs don't work as well for them.

**See** Antiepileptic Medicines.

## Phenytoin

Phenytoin is the name of the chemical used in the drug Epanutin®.

**See** Antiepileptic Medicines.

## Photosensitivity

Some people are affected by certain types of lighting which causes them to have seizures. This affects more girls than boys. The lighting may be from a television set, computer video games, from the lights of a disco or from any other flickering light.

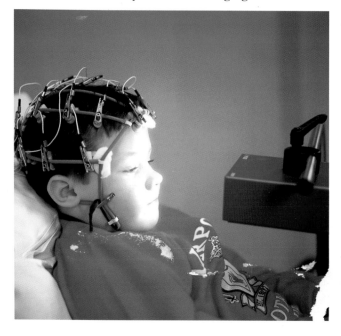

What happens is that the flickering light triggers part of the brain into acting abnormally. This causes the seizure. A flashing light is used during an E.E.G. test to see if the person is affected by flickering lights. If the E.E.G. shows abnormal activity during the flashing light test then this is called photosensitivity. It is not common amongst people with epilepsy, and it hardly ever occurs in people without epilepsy. It is sometimes seen in people with generalised seizures.

Only a small number of all people who have seizures have them as a result of flickering lights.

If watching the television causes you to have seizures, it is helpful to sit as far away

from the screen as possible (at least a metre) and to have a lamp on top of the television set. If you use a computer it is unwise to use an ordinary television screen as the display. Proper computer monitors are much better and cause very few problems.

If you play video games on a television set, it is sensible to sit at least one metre from the screen and to have other lights on in the room. Video games should not be played by people who have photosensitive epilepsy when they are very tired.

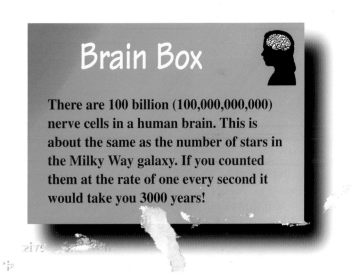

There is not a lot that can be done about the flashing lights of a disco other than to keep well away from the lights even if it means not going to the disco.

## Brain Box

There are 100 billion (100,000,000,000) nerve cells in a human brain. This is about the same as the number of stars in the Milky Way galaxy. If you counted them at the rate of one every second it would take you 3000 years!

# Physical Education (PE)

PE is very good for all children, including those with epilepsy.  There are very few parts of a PE lesson that a child with epilepsy should not join in.  One example is climbing up wall bars or ropes.

# Pre-menstrual Epilepsy

As young girls mature they start to have monthly periods. Those with a tendency towards epilepsy can have seizures before or at the start of each period.  Nobody  really knows why this can happen. It could be due to a change in the balance of fluids in the body, which can affect the brain.

On the other hand, it could be to do with a change in the balance of hormones within the body.

## Prognosis

Prognosis means how doctors think that a person's epilepsy (or any other condition) will progress. If they think that in the future a person's seizures will be well controlled then the prognosis is good. If, however, the outlook is for the seizures to increase or get no better then the prognosis is poor. Most people with epilepsy will have a good prognosis.

## Pseudo Seizures

These are not epileptic seizures at all. The word "pseudo" means false and this is exactly what they are - false seizures.

The person shows all the signs of having a seizure but is imitating a real seizure. The most likely reason for this happening is that the person, for some reason, is trying to attract attention.

Sometimes pseudo seizures are very difficult to recognise because they can look like true seizures.

## Research

It takes a long time and many, many millions of pounds before a new antiepileptic medicine is ready to be used to control seizures.

Every day some of the cleverest scientists and doctors in the world are working to develop these new drugs. Many scientific discoveries happen by accident, while others are the result of many years of painstaking work.

Researchers take every possible care to make sure that a new drug is safe before it can be given to people. Volunteers are used to test the new drugs to see how well they work and what side effects, if any, there might be. If these trials are successful then, after a lot of careful procedures have been followed, the drug becomes available for doctors to prescribe.

One thing is sure - new drugs will always be developed, and so the outlook for people with epilepsy gets better all the time.

## Rivotril®

Rivotril® is the trade name for the drug clonazepam. It is taken as small white tablets and used in the treatment of myoclonic, absence and partial seizures.

See Antiepileptic Medicines.

## Sabril®

Sabril® is the trade name for the drug vigabatrin. It is used alone or alongside other antiepileptic tablets when the doctor is finding it difficult to control seizures. It is also used to treat infantile spasms. The tablets are the same shape as a rugby ball and are white. Sabril® can also be taken as a powder which is dissolved in water, juice or milk and taken as a drink.

See Antiepileptic Medicines.

## Saint Mark

Saint Mark wrote some of the Bible. In Chapter 9 (Verses 14 -19) of his writings in the New Testament part he gives a very accurate description of a tonic-clonic seizure. This shows that epilepsy is nothing new - it has been with us for as long as there have been people on Earth.

This piece of writing also shows how important it is to care for the parent as well as the child.

## Secondarily Generalised Seizures

Sometimes somebody might have a partial seizure and then go on to have a generalised seizure. If this happens, the generalised seizure would usually take the form of an atonic, tonic, clonic or tonic-clonic seizure. When somebody has a partial seizure which leads on to a generalised seizure, doctors call it a secondarily generalised seizure.

## Seizure

People often talk about somebody having "fits", "funny turns", "attacks" and even "wobblers". Now you've read them, forget them! The correct term is seizure, which comes from a Greek word meaning "to take hold of".

A seizure happens when part of the brain stops working properly for a short time. When the brain is operating properly, tiny amounts of electricity rush around from place to place, making everything work normally. During a seizure some of the electricity goes a bit haywire, so that the part of the brain where this is happening doesn't work in the right way. Actually, it might only be a small part of the brain that is affected, or it might be most of it. This means that there are many different types of seizure, depending on which part of the brain is affected. Obviously, if any part of the brain stops working properly, even for a short time, then this can cause some unusual things to happen to the person having the seizure. The person might twitch and jerk, or go blank for a few seconds, or even fall to the ground, perhaps with convulsions. It is even possible that strange noises or music might be heard, or the person might experience a strange smell or taste. It just depends on what part of the brain is having the seizure.

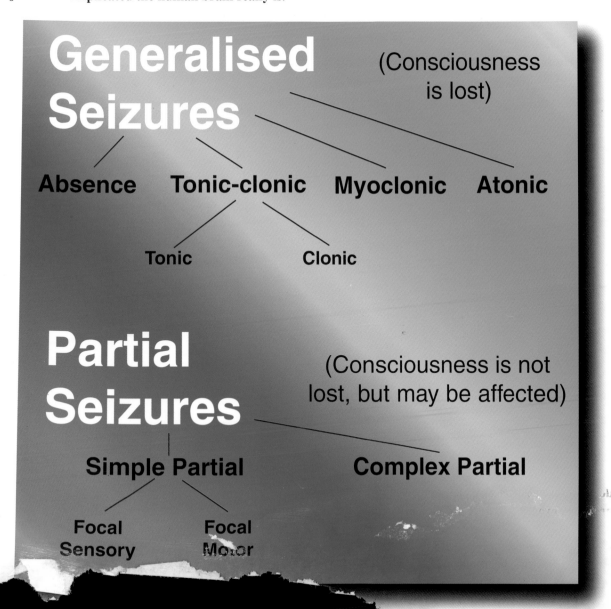

Doctors group (or classify) all the known seizures into a few main types. There are generalised seizures and partial seizures. Generalised seizures, which affect the whole brain, are spilt up into tonic-clonic, absence, myoclonic, atonic and clonic seizures. Anybody who has a generalised seizure loses consciousness during the seizure. Partial seizures, which only affect part of the brain, are split up into two main types: complex partial and simple partial seizures. Simple partial seizures are further split up into focal motor and focal sensory seizures. People who have a partial seizure don't lose consciousness, but their consciousness may still be affected. There are actually many other types of seizure. This shows just how complicated the human brain really is.

**Generalised Seizures** (Consciousness is lost)

Absence    Tonic-clonic    Myoclonic    Atonic

Tonic    Clonic

**Partial Seizures** (Consciousness is not lost, but may be affected)

Simple Partial    Complex Partial

Focal Sensory    Focal Motor

## Seizure Diary

A seizure diary is a simple chart or a small book for keeping a record of seizures. It is very useful for noting the dates of seizures and for writing a brief description of what actually happened during a seizure. Noting the date is easy but a witness usually has to give the information about what actually happened.

The diary of events helps the doctor to get to the root of the problem and to decide the best treatment.

Some people, as well as keeping a diary, make arrangements for themselves to be videoed on a camcorder when a seizure occurs. If a video recording can be made then the doctor may find it very useful. The doctor may then be able to tell precisely what sort of seizure someone is having. This will then help the doctor to prescribe the best treatment.

## Side Effects

These are the unwanted effects of all drugs and medicines. Although drugs are used to cure and control illness, they can also cause problems themselves.

example, penicillin is a widely cure infection but it can cause a rash in some le.

is a drug that some e of them can have blems. Thousands

Like any other drugs, antiepileptic medicine can cause side effects and people taking it should find out what the possible side effects are so that they can be aware of any likely problem. Fortunately, the side effects are generally quite harmless and most people don't suffer any side-effects at all.

People should ask their hospital doctor, family doctor or pharmacist (chemist) about these side effects.

## Simple Partial Seizures

In a simple partial seizure there is no loss of consciousness. During the seizure the person remains completely aware of what is happening. They are different from complex partial seizures because the person's consciousness is not affected at all. Simple partial seizures, like complex partial seizures, are different from generalised seizures because only part of the brain is affected.

There are many different types of simple partial seizures. It could be that an arm or leg may jerk (focal motor seizure) or there could be a numbness or tingling in a part of the body or a strange taste or smell (focal sensory seizure). The most common type of simple partial seizure, however, is an aura.

The abnormal electrical discharge is happening in a single part of the brain and so, for example, if it is in the part of the brain which controls the left arm then the problem will occur in the left arm.

## Sodium Valproate

Sodium valproate is the name of the chemical used in the drug Epilim®.

See Antiepileptic Medicines.

## SOS Talisman

This is piece of jewellery such as necklace or bracelet which contains a piece of paper. People who wear a Talisn write all necessary information about the piece of pape

# S

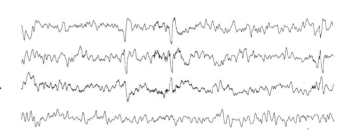

## Spike and Sharp Wave

This is an E.E.G. pattern which often shows up if a trace is done on somebody with epilepsy. However, not everybody with epilepsy produces these patterns, so the doctor still relies very much on a description of what is happening in a seizure before deciding that epilepsy is the problem.

## Spike and Slow Wave

This is an E.E.G. pattern which is usually seen in children with absence seizures who have 'petit mal' epilepsy. It may also be seen in other generalised seizures.

## Sport and Leisure Activities

Children with epilepsy can do nearly all sports. Team games such as football, netball and tennis are enjoyed by many thousands of children who have the condition. There are stars of sport who have epilepsy, and there is no reason why children who are good at sport, and who have epilepsy, should not be tomorrow's stars.

Some sports are obviously dangerous for people with epilepsy. For example, deep sea diving is not advisable and neither is steep mountain or rock climbing. The number of sports that can be enjoyed is far greater than those which are unsuitable.

If there is a sport you want to do it is important to ask the hospital doctor how suitable it is.

# Status Epilepticus

This is when a seizure continues for a long time or when one seizure follows another without the person regaining consciousness in between. It is a dangerous condition and needs special and urgent treatment.

So, if a seizure lasts for longer than 5 minutes, or there are groups of seizures without the person regaining consciousness in between, the person is in danger of going into status epilepticus. An ambulance should be called to get the person to hospital, where the seizure can be stopped by giving certain drugs.

The drugs are given by doctors or specially trained people. One of these drugs is called diazepam or Stesolid®.

# Swimming

Every child who has epilepsy should learn how to swim. Special precautions might be needed but these are easy and straightforward. The main thing is to make sure that there is somebody on the side of the

swimming pool who can make a rescue in case a seizure happens. The pool attendant should be told by the swimmer about the epilepsy so that an eye can be kept on the situation.

Whereas swimming in a supervised pool is fine for people with epilepsy, it is unwise for them to go swimming in the open sea, where there could be strong currents and tides. This can make rescue dangerous or even impossible.

## Teenager Clinics

Children under the age of 16 years usually attend a local children's hospital or children's department to receive help to control epilepsy. As they become teenagers they may feel uncomfortable attending these clinics because there are other children there who are much younger than themselves. Often they don't look forward to hospital appointments and sometimes don't go to the clinic at all. To get over this, clinics just for teenagers are held in many areas. At these Teenager Clinics the young people are introduced to the neurologist who will be looking after them when they reach 16 or 17 years of age. Although this neurologist won't be treating the teenager just yet, he or she will discuss the patient's progress with the paediatric neurologist. The two doctors will plan the future treatment of their patient.

## Tegretol®

Tegretol® is the trade name for the drug carbamazepine. It is taken as an ordinary tablet or as a chewable tablet. Ordinary tablets are white and the chewable ones are orange-coloured. It can also be taken as a white liquid which tastes of caramel. It is used in the treatment of both generalised and partial seizures.

See Antiepileptic Medicines.

## Tegretol Retard®

These tablets are designed to release the drug carbamazepine slowly throughout the day. The lower dosed tablet is pale orange in colour and the higher dosed tablet is coloured brick red. It is used in the treatment of both generalised and partial seizures.

See Antiepileptic Medicines.

# Telemetry

Telemetry means using a closed circuit video camera which is linked to an E.E.G. machine. This is so that the doctor can watch what is happening to the patient while the E.E.G. is being recorded. One half of the TV screen shows a picture of the patient and the other half shows the E.E.G. pattern. So, if a seizure happens, the camera will record what effect this has on the person, and the E.E.G. records the brainwaves.

This is a great help because the person can be viewed over long periods and even throughout the night. Once the testing is completed, the doctor can play the recordings back to see what exactly has been going on.

The video camera monitors the patient while the E.E.G. records the brainwaves.

The screen displays the patient and the E.E.G. trace at the same time.

## Brain Box

The brain makes up only about one fiftieth of our body weight but it uses up a quarter of all the oxygen that the body needs.

It is no surprise that, since our brains rely so much on oxygen, too little or too much oxygen can have very unpleasant effects on our consciousness.

## Temporal Lobe Epilepsy/Seizures

See Complex Partial Seizures.

## Brain Box

The fastest messages which travel along the nervous system reach 288 km/h (180 mph). This slows down as we get older.

## Therapeutic Ranges

Doctors know how much of a drug should be in the blood for it to work best. This amount is called the therapeutic range of the drug. If the amount of the drug in the bloodstream is outside the therapeutic range it means that there is too much drug or not enough. A simple blood test can show up how much of the drug is present in the person's bloodstream. If the doctor thinks that the test might be necessary it can be done at the hospital during a normal clinic. Most people with epilepsy do not need to have this blood test done.

## Tonic Seizures

If you had a tonic seizure then your muscles would stiffen and, if you were standing up, you would fall over. There is a good chance that this would injure you. People who have regular tonic seizures are advised to wear a protective helmet. A tonic seizure is a type of generalised seizure.

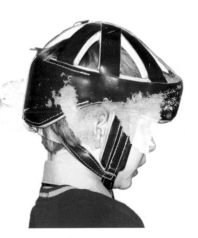

# TV

## Tonic-clonic Seizures

This is the proper name for what some people call "Grand Mal" seizures. Most people who have heard of epilepsy usually think of somebody having a tonic-clonic seizure.

If you had a tonic-clonic seizure then it would probably start with you crying out, then going unconscious. You would, of course, fall down. You would go stiff (tonic stage) then your muscles would start twitching (clonic stage). As the muscles twitch it is possible that the bladder will empty if it is full. Finally, you would recover, but you might be confused and dazed. You might want to sleep, and you might have a headache for a while.

A person watching such a seizure may notice the lips turning blue and, if the tongue has been bitten, blood may be seen to trickle from the mouth. A normal amount of saliva is produced, but the person is not able to swallow it, so it collects in the mouth and foams. This can look very alarming, although there is really not much danger.

The whole seizure usually lasts 2 - 5 minutes. A tonic-clonic seizure is a type of generalised seizure.

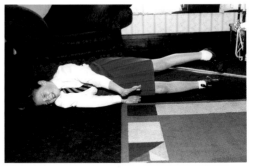

During the tonic phase the body goes stiff.

In the clonic phase the limbs jerk out of control.

## Triggers

A trigger is something which makes it more likely for a person with epilepsy to have seizures. Some examples of triggers are: not taking tablets regularly, tiredness, menstrual periods, hyperventilation, flashing lights and high body temperature.

## Van Boyer

He was a German scientist who discovered using phenobarbitone. He found that it was very good at calming people down and from 1886 to 1912 it was used only to make people relaxed. In 1912 a doctor called Hauptman used it to control seizures.

## Vigabatrin

Vigabatrin is the name of the chemical used in the drug Sabril®.

See Antiepileptic Medicines.

# Van Gogh (1853 - 1890)

Vincent van Gogh was born in the Netherlands (Holland). He started off being a preacher, but soon turned to painting beautiful pictures. In 1886 he left Holland to live in France where, between 1888 and 1890, he painted his most famous pictures. The best known of all his pictures is the Sunflowers, which is worth many millions of pounds.

As well as being one of the greatest artists ever Vincent van Gogh happened to have epilepsy.

"Self-Portrait" - 1887

"Sunflowers"

"Outdoor Cafe at Night" - 1888

# Wada Test

A Japanese neurologist called Doctor Wada invented a special test which is now named after him.

This test is done if there is a chance that an operation might stop some complex partial seizures. It is used to find out whether the operation would affect every day actions like speaking. This is because your brain controls speech. The part of the brain that controls speech is in the left temporal lobe in most people - but it could be in the right temporal lobe. If the seizures are caused by damage in the temporal lobe controlling speech, then the surgeon won't want to operate to stop the seizures because this might affect the person's ability to talk.

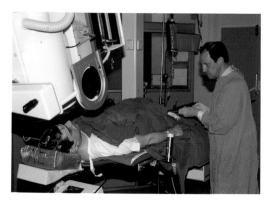

One side of the brain is put to sleep for a short while, using a special injection.

One half of the brain is put to sleep using a medicine. The other side is still awake (so the person is still awake). The doctor asks the person questions to see how well the awake part of the brain is working. After a while, the test is done again on the other side of the brain (you can be totally awake with only one half of your brain working). If the person is able to talk properly, then the side of the brain that is awake must be controlling the person's ability to talk. If the person isn't able to talk properly, then the side of the brain that is awake doesn't control speech - the part that controls speech must be asleep.

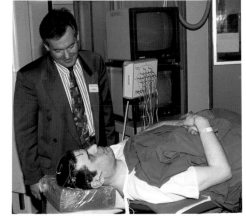

The doctor tests the patient to see if speech is impaired.

Very few children have this test because very few need to have surgery to treat their epilepsy.

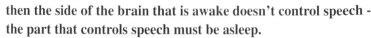

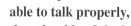

, the

it

## Withdrawal Seizures

People who have been taking antiepileptic medicines for many years, and have not had a seizure for a very long time, sometimes decide to stop taking their drugs. Their bodies have become so used to the drugs that there is a risk that seizures will start again. These seizures are called withdrawal seizures because of the withdrawal of the drugs. They usually only happen if the drug is withdrawn very quickly. If the drug is withdrawn very slowly, over a couple of months, then withdrawal seizures do not usually happen.

## X-Rays

Ordinary X-Rays used to look at broken bones are of no use in trying to find out the cause of epilepsy. Special X-Rays used in a CAT Scanner, however, can sometimes be very useful in helping the doctor to find the fault in the brain causing the seizures.

## Zarontin®

Zarontin® is a trade name for the drug ethosuximide. It can either be taken as a blackcurrant or orange-flavoured syrup or as a soft orange capsule. It is used to treat absence seizures and sometimes myoclonic seizures.

See Antiepileptic Medicines.